PHOTOGRAPHY

David Cumming

The Arts

Architecture
Dance
Design
Literature
Music
Painting and Sculpture
Photography
Theatre
The Cinema

Cover illustration: Many photographs are made up
from ordinary objects like this building in Texas.
However, by capturing the reflection of the sky in its
glass walls, a beautiful, slightly unreal image is
created.

Series Editor: Rosemary Ashley
Editor: Penny Horton
Designer: David Armitage
Consultant: David Chandler, Exhibitions Officer,
Photographers Gallery, London

First published in 1989 by
Wayland (Publishers) Limited
61 Western Road, Hove
East Sussex BN3 1JD, England

British Library Cataloguing in Publication Data
Cumming, David
  Photography.—(The arts).
  1. Photography
  I. Title   II. Series
  770

  ISBN 1–85210–455–4

Typeset by DP Press, Sevenoaks, England
Printed and bound in Italy by Sagdos

Contents

1 Is it Art?

Photography comes from the Greek words *photos* meaning light and *graphos* meaning drawing, so it literally means 'drawing with light'. The word was first used in 1839 by Sir John Herschel, a British scientist, in a lecture he gave entitled, 'The Art of Photography, or The Application of the Chemical Rays of Light to the Purpose of Pictorial Representation.' It is interesting to note that Herschel referred to photography as an 'art'.

For a long time, arguments about whether photography was technical or artistic held back its development; but then, in its early days, it involved complex exposure calculations and lengthy and intricate darkroom processes. It is hardly surprising in view of these technicalities that people thought that photography belonged more to the world of scientists than artists. Artists, too, resented the ease with which photography could make pictures of the world much more quickly and with more detail than they ever could, so they tried to dismiss it as something which needed no talent. Photographers retaliated by producing photographs similar in style to paintings, assuming that if paintings were artistic, then photographs like them would be considered as art. Indeed, this did bring them respectability and acceptance in society and with this confidence, boosted by lighter

Many things happen too fast for our eyes to notice them. Today's cameras have the ability to 'freeze' action, revealing, for example, the fascinating process of a kingfisher catching a fish.

and easier-to-use equipment, photographers began to establish their own way of looking at the world, one that would eventually exist totally independently of painters and their art.

However, it has been argued that because photographs are produced by a machine, photography cannot be seen as an art. A machine has no brain – it cannot think or imagine. So, does photography belong in the science laboratory: to a world of exact measurements and calculations, where there are right and wrong ways of doing things; where opinions count for little and experiments prove that one person's views are correct and another person's are incorrect? Surely using a machine means that photography is not an art, but a science? For instance, if two photographers, side by side, photograph a view, they will both produce the same image. But if two painters paint the same view, their images will be totally different. In art, opinions vary; in science, there is only one solution to a problem. Does this not mean that photography is a science?

Photography is a medium of expression, a way of conveying ideas, and the camera is its tool. A painter's tool is traditionally a brush, but some are now using computers to create pictures. Writers, too, use typewriters and word processors in their work. If artists like these can use machines and yet still be thought of as artists, why not photographers? The camera, after all, is only a means of 'drawing with light'; the real photographic process happens inside the camera, when rays of light react on a film's chemicals to produce an image which can be turned into a picture. This is a chemical reaction. But a photographer *can* control this process by choosing how much light hits the film and, with the aid of filters, alter the quality of the light.

Above *A detail from a collage by Laszlo Moholy-Nagy (see also page 19) in 1923. It combines traditional art, with the use of airbrush, pen and ink and what was then a modern art form: the photograph.*

Both of these affect the chemical reaction and hence the image that it produces. So, photography is an art, but also a science.

Artists can decide how much art or science is going to appear in their work. The work can be purely imagined, bearing little relation to reality, reflecting only the artist's inner world, or it can be realistic – something that has required no imagination: a true reflection of the real world. Thus, an illustrator can use a pen to draw either an imaginative picture of a building or an architect's plan. .A photographer, too, has this choice. He or she can take a straightforward photograph of a building or create an image from the patterns and shapes made by reflections in its windows or shadows formed by its walls. A photographer needs to possess both artistic and technical skills. There are no rules about what is worth looking at and what is not; it is up to the individual to decide what he or she wants to 'capture' through the lens. But there are rules about how people record what they see. Photographers need to know how cameras, lenses, films and filters work, to be able to communicate what they see. So the required technical skills are needed as well as artistic talent.

Today, no one questions photography's role in society. We live in a visual world, one in which information is conveyed to us through our

Above *Automatic, compact cameras have helped to turn photography into a worldwide hobby, which is now practised by millions of people of all ages.*

eyes via newspapers, magazines, television, books, brochures, posters — the list is infinite. Photography plays an enormous part in this process, helping to influence our ideas about ourselves, our friends and even things we cannot see. Once cameras were bulky boxes that had to be supported by tripods; now they are so small and sophisticated that they can provide us with pictures from almost anywhere: from outer space to inside the human body. Photography itself, once the hobby of a select minority who could afford it, is now a profession which is backed by a worldwide industry. Cameras, lenses and all their accessories are mass-produced, frequently in their millions. It is also a favourite pastime of people around the world. In western countries, most families own a camera; most shopping centres either offer a photographic shop or one where films can be processed in only one hour. We have cameras that do everything for themselves; cameras that provide photographs a minute after they have been taken; even disposable cameras which can be thrown away once the film is finished. Camera manufacturers are now looking at electronic ways of producing photographs, using a disk or a tape. The filmless camera is on the way. But enough of the future, let us go back to the beginning of photography when all this was unimagineable.

2 'From today painting is dead'

August 1839, Paris: a hushed audience of French scholars and scientists heard the news that a fellow countryman, Louis Daguerre, had invented a new way of producing pictures, which used neither pencils nor paint – just the effect of light on certain chemicals. No sooner had the speaker finished than the room emptied as people hurried off to tell their friends about this wonderful discovery. Within hours, shops all over the capital had sold out of the equipment needed for the 'daguerreotype process', as it was called. During the next few days, keen daguerreotypists could be seen practising their new hobby in the streets of Paris, while painters looked on anxiously, worried for their futures. 'From today painting is dead,' muttered the artist Paul Delaroche gloomily, after being shown one of these new daguerreotypes.

Daguerre was not the first person to notice that light changed the colour of some chemicals; nor was he the first to develop a process to use this to create pictures, but he was certainly the first person to announce his discovery and also the first to come up with a process that was not too complicated.

In fact, the beginnings of photography can be traced back to the eleventh century. At this time, people noticed that, if a small hole in one wall was the only source of light in a room, a dim picture of the scene outside would appear on the opposite wall. A room like this was called a *camera obscura*, meaning 'dark chamber' in Latin.

In the fifteenth century, an Italian scientist went one step further and obtained a clearer, brighter picture by putting a lens from a telescope in the hole in the wall.

By the 1600s the *camera obscura* had become popular with artists, who traced round the image produced by the lens to make accurate drawings of buildings and views. No longer a room in a building, they were now portable, either in the form of a large box which the photographer could sit inside (a converted sedan-chair, for instance) or a collapsible tent. Often, the lens was mounted in the roof and, with the help of a mirror, the image appeared on a table beneath. Then, in 1685, a German monk named Johann Zahn, designed a miniature version of the *camera obscura*. This was a box, 60 cm long and 22 cm high, with an adjustable lens at one end which, through a mirror, projected an image on to a screen on the top. In many ways, it resembled what was to be later called a camera.

So, by the end of the seventeenth century there was a box which, with some minor modifications, could be used for taking a picture. All that was needed now was a way of preserving the image. The first

Above *Louis Daguerre (1787–1851), the Frenchman whose process for making daguerreotypes laid the foundations for what came to be called photography. The French government granted him a pension for life as a reward for his achievements, on condition that he told the world about his discovery.*

Above right *This is the oldest daguerreotype in existence. It was taken in 1837 by Louis Daguerre, two years before he announced his photographic discovery to the people of Paris.*

Below right *This illustration shows how a small hole in a darkened room can project an upside-down picture of the scene outside on the opposite wall. The* camera obscura, *as it is called, was discovered in the twelfth century and was the first step towards photography.*

steps towards this were taken in 1727, when Johann Heinrich Schulze, a German scientist, noticed that silver nitrate turned dark in sunlight. He had discovered what we call a light-sensitive chemical. But it was not until the beginning of the nineteenth century that the idea of using it in a camera came to light.

Around 1800, Thomas Wedgwood, the son of a famous British potter, started dipping paper into silver nitrate and putting it into a camera. Unfortunately, the light was too weak and Wedgwood too impatient, so no image appeared. Had he left the paper longer in his camera, he would have obtained an image and might now be thought of as the inventor of photography.

As it was, this honour fell to a Frenchman called Nicéphore Niépce. In 1816, he began experimenting with cameras, trying to record the view from his window on paper which had been soaked in silver chloride. He succeeded in producing the world's first black-and-white 'negative' – a picture of everything in reverse, with what should be white shown as black and vice versa. However, Niépce wanted a 'positive', a picture showing the world as it really was, so he began looking at other ways of making a photograph. In 1826, he put a sheet of metal, coated with a tar-like substance, in his camera for eight hours. The result was the first photograph. Unfortunately, his process was too complicated to have a future.

One of the few people who heard about Niépce's success was Louis Daguerre, a talented artist who soon became fascinated by photographs. He and Niépce became friends and then formed a business to develop Niépce's ideas. Niépce died shortly afterwards, leaving Daguerre to carry on and discover his own way of making photographs. He produced his first pictures in 1835, but it was not until 1837 that he found a way of 'fixing' them, that is, stopping the whole of the paper going dark when you looked at it in the light.

One of the world's oldest surviving photographs. It was taken in 1824 by Nicéphore Niépce (1765–1833) who produced the first photograph. Unfortunately his process was too complicated to have widespread use and he died before he could simplify it.

The French Government was delighted with his discovery and awarded Daguerre a life-long pension on condition that he made his process known to the rest of the world.

When the daguerreotype process was made public in 1839, Henry Fox Talbot, a brilliant British mathematician and scientist, must have been a very disappointed man. He had been working on his own method for the previous five years and now, just as the end was in sight, news reached him of Daguerre's discovery. Spurred on by Daguerre's success, Fox Talbot produced his own pictures in 1840. He called them 'calotypes', after the Greek word for beautiful, *kalos*. While the end result was the same, Daguerre's and Fox Talbot's methods were different. A calotype was made from a paper negative, which had been pressed against another piece of paper, coated with light-sensitive chemicals and put in the sun: the negative image was printed as a positive one on the second sheet of paper. A daguerreotype, however, was produced by light acting on chemicals on top of a sheet of copper, forming a positive picture. Of the two, Fox Talbot's discovery was the more important as it is still used in photography today.

Each process had its advantages and disadvantages. Calotypes were slow to produce and were not so detailed, but copies could be made of their negatives. Daguerreotypes were very clear and could be produced quickly, but each one was unique. Ideally, a process that combined the best of both was wanted: a way of producing good pictures from re-usable negatives.

In 1851, Frederick Scott Archer, a British sculptor and professional photographer, realized that collodion had a use in photography. Collodion was a sticky liquid that dried into a hard, clear film, and Archer began to use it to coat a sheet of glass, or plate as it came to be called, then covering this layer with chemicals that would stick to the collodion. When exposed to light in a camera, a negative image was produced on the plate, which would produce a sharp, positive picture on a piece of paper. The only problem was that the picture had to be taken and developed while the collodion was still wet – a messy job which meant that a portable darkroom had to be carried about by the photographer. Even so, the results were good enough for photographers to switch from using the daguerreotype and calotype processes to this new collodion method.

The search was now on for a process that would use dry plates, so that a photographer could take pictures away from the darkroom without being weighed down by masses of equipment. During the 1860s, it seemed that hardly a month went by without someone suggesting a new idea that was just as quickly forgotten. Then, in 1871, a discovery was made which marked the beginning of the system we still use. Richard Maddox, a British doctor and keen photographer, replaced the collodion layer on the plates with gelatin. It worked just as well, and could be used when it was dry. And if it could be used on glass, then why not on paper?

Henry Fox Talbot (1800–77) invented the calotype process, which he revealed in 1841. In 1844, he published a book entitled The Pencil of Nature. *It was the first book to be illustrated with photographs, in which this photograph appeared.*

An American, called George Eastman, decided to try this method, producing the first roll of paper film in 1885. Being a clever businessman, he wanted as many people as possible to buy it, so in 1888, he brought out a very simple, small roll-film camera that anyone could use. He called it the Kodak, a name he was to use on all his other photographic products and which was to become famous throughout the world. The Kodak was an immediate success and opened up photography to millions of enthusiastic amateurs around the world. The following year, Eastman replaced paper roll film with a plastic film, very similar to the one we use today.

At the end of the nineteenth century, many of the things we now take for granted were in use, such as easy-to-use, hand-held cameras, easy-to-load roll films, and flashguns (using magnesium powder, which gives out a very bright flash when it is ignited). By then, people understood all the scientific rules and laws which affected the way in which photographic chemicals and equipment worked: there was little else to learn or discover. So, while the nineteenth century was a time of invention in photography, the twentieth century has been one of improvement. There have been no discoveries to equal those of the previous century; instead, we have modified nineteenth-century inventions, taking advantage of developments in industry and science to make cameras easier to use, more efficient and much smaller.

In the two areas of film and camera design, things have advanced greatly during the twentieth century. At the turn of the century, although people realized how colour photography worked, no one had found a way of putting their ideas into practice. In 1907, the Autochrome process was invented by the Lumière brothers in France.

A photographer at work on Clapham Common, London, in 1873. He is loading a 'plate' into his camera. Once exposed, this would be developed in his portable darkroom on the hand cart. By the late nineteenth century, there were many portrait photographers, but the process was still too complicated and the equipment too bulky for it to be a widespread hobby.

It was the first uncomplicated method of producing colour photographs, and entailed placing a layer of tiny, coloured grains of starch on top of a coating of light-sensitive chemicals on a glass plate. The black and white positive image produced in the chemicals appeared coloured when the plate was held up to the light. But it was not until 1936, with the arrival of Kodachrome, that the first real colour pictures were taken. Manufactured by the Kodak company, this was the first colour film to have layers of chemicals sensitive to blue, green and red light, from which all other colours can be made. In processing, the different layers combine to form a bright, sharp positive picture. An improved version of this film is used today.

As far as cameras were concerned, the appearance of the Leica in 1925 caused an enormous stir in photographic circles, because it was so small. This reduction in size had been achieved by using the narrow 35 mm film of movie cameras. To begin with, other manufacturers were reluctant to follow the Leica example as the pictures obtained from the small negatives were not as sharp as those from roll films. However, improvements in the quality of 35 mm films in the 1930s and 1940s changed their minds and, by the 1950s, most manufacturers accepted that the future lay in cameras that used 35 mm film.

This beautiful autochrome picture was taken in 1920 by the famous French photographer, Jacques Henri Lartigue. Invented by the Lumière brothers in France in the early 1900s, the autochrome process was the first successful method of producing colour photographs.

13

Far right *The amazing advances that have been achieved in the twentieth century include the ability to take sharp, detailed photographs underwater.*

Inset *An historic moment captured on film: an astronaut from the Apollo 11 spacecraft raises the American flag on the moon in 1969.*

A photographer using a Leica camera, could look above the lens at the view he or she wanted to take. With the new range of 35 mm cameras, the photographer could look through the lens: something that was very useful because different types of lenses could now be used. These were called single lens reflex cameras (SLRs). Their high price meant that they were mainly for professional photographers while the amateurs had to make do with roll-film cameras that ranged from simple-to-use boxes to more complex, folding models, which could be adjusted for different light conditions.

The arrival of the Kodak Instamatic in the early 1960s signalled the end of roll-film cameras for amateurs. The film for these new cameras came in a cartridge, which simply dropped into the back. Other manufacturers followed suit or switched to 35 mm films, as they had done for their more advanced SLRs. The 1960s also saw the introduction of electronics into photography, because batteries had become small enough to fit into camera bodies. Cameras now became increasingly automatic, with built-in exposure meters that measured the strength of the light and then made the appropriate adjustments to the shutter speed or the size of the lens aperture. Cameras also became cheaper as manufacturers began to use mass-production techniques in their factories and amateurs could now afford to buy SLRs. As electricity became more important in the workings of a camera, replacing levers and springs, the way was open for a computer to take charge of everything.

In 1976, the Canon AE-1 appeared in our shops. Inside it, the electrical system was controlled by a computer. Ten years later, this complex machine seemed very basic by the side of a camera of the 1980s, with its flashing lights, buzzers and panels displaying all sorts of information. Now, all a photographer needs to do is press the shutter button and the camera will do the rest – select the correct shutter speed and aperture (warning its operator to use a flash if there is not enough light), focus itself and wind the film on. Yet, today's cameras are as easy to operate as Eastman's Kodak of 1888 and use the same principles as the eleventh-century *camera obscura*.

Through the development of photography and science, satellites like Voyager *can send us photographs from deep in space, such as this one of the distant planet Uranus.*

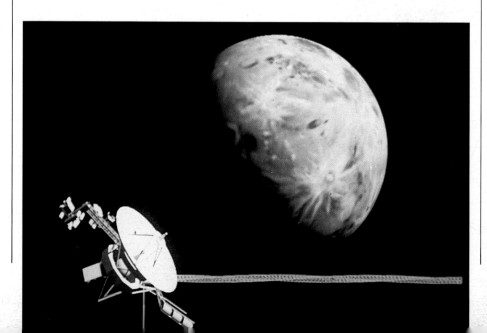

3 Ways of Seeing

'Tears, idle tears, I know not what they mean'. This photograph, taken by Julia Margaret Cameron (1815–79) in 1875, was part of a series of pictures commissioned by the poet Alfred Tennyson to illustrate a volume of his poems.

In the 1850s, photographic societies were springing up in many British cities. Keen to be seen as artists, their members put on exhibitions and invited art critics for their opinions. The critics were not impressed. They thought the photographs of everyday scenes were ugly and dull, and because they had been produced by a machine, the critics could not accept photography as art.

Crestfallen, photographers returned to their studios to ponder their next move. If pictures of the real world were not art, perhaps they should use their imaginations to produce ones similar to the paintings which were popular at that time. Surely, then, photography would be considered artistic and not merely a mechanical means of recording life.

At this time, the Pre-Raphaelite Brotherhood began to exert an influence on British painting. The Pre-Raphaelites were dissatisfied with nineteenth-century painting styles and had revived the themes and techniques of fifteenth-century Italian artists. They produced large, extremely detailed pictures with a story or a message, using ideas from poems, novels and history. Although the Pre-Raphaelites disbanded in the mid-1850s, their work continued to have a great influence on other painters and on the way Victorians looked at pictures and, hence, photography.

So, criticized for taking pictures of the real world, photographers created imaginary ones, similar to the Pre-Raphaelites', in their studios. These were transformed into stage sets, complete with actors, elaborate scenery, costumes and props all carefully positioned according to a plan of the final photograph. If all this proved too much for the space available, then each part of the scene was photographed separately and all the negatives matched up for the final print. Such composite pictures demanded a lot of the photographer, both in time and skill; nevertheless, many thought it worth the effort. One such photographer was Oscar Rejlander, himself a painter, whose picture *Two Ways of Life*, illustrating good and bad behaviour, needed thirty negatives. After all that work, a gallery in Scotland considered its 'bad' aspects too shocking and covered half the picture with a black cloth. However, the whole of it was shown to Queen Victoria in 1857 as a work of art.

For many photographers this was enough for them to feel that they were recognized as artists. Others were not so satisfied – artists they might well be, but only because they had copied the styles and ideas of painters. For photographers to be true artists, they would have to establish their own ways of creating pictures, totally separate from

painters' methods. These photographers also felt that they should be given more freedom to develop their individual talents and not be tied by strict rules about what was a good picture and what was not.

This feeling spread during the 1870s as photography, now cheaper and less complicated, became increasingly popular. Many of these 'new' photographers wanted to show their work in exhibitions and objected to photographic societies' restrictions which prevented them from doing so. The demands for more freedom of expression and for photography to stand on its own feet, without any help from painters, prompted some photographers to break away from the societies and form their own groups. Their members were given the collective title of 'Pictorialists'.

Above Two Ways of Life, *a composite photograph by Oscar Rejlander (1813–75) created in 1875. He used over thirty different pictures to achieve the final image, photographing people either individually or in carefully positioned groups. It was very popular, copies of it even being bought by the British royal family.*

Left
Charming portraits taken by Julia Margaret Cameron in 1865. She took up photography in 1864 at the age of forty-nine and mainly used the collodion process. She was often criticized for not conforming to the styles of her contemporaries. Today she is seen as very talented and ahead of her time.

In their determination to make photography an art in its own right, the Pictorialists thought a picture's most important appeal should be its beauty. What it was about and whether it contained a message were of secondary importance. To encourage people to think of a photograph as beautiful, all its detail and sharp outlines were often softened with a special lens, or even by the photographer shaking the tripod which supported the camera. Some Pictorialists also took advantage of new processing methods to produce photographs that looked as though they had been painted with a brush or drawn in crayon or charcoal. Others 'touched up' negatives, altering their details, to get the effects they wanted. In their new approach to photography, the Pictorialists were influenced by changes in painting styles. In Britain, Turner and Whistler, and in France, Impressionist painters like Monet and Degas, were turning away from the highly detailed, message-bearing pictures of the Pre-Raphaelites to a style that conveyed a mood or atmosphere by the use of different tones of colour and indistinct shapes.

In the 1890s, some Pictorialists swung away from their rather romantic view of the world to one offering a more accurate representation of reality. This was prompted by the publication of *Naturalistic Photography for Students of the Art* in 1889. Its author, Peter Emerson, a British doctor turned photographer, called for 'beautiful' pictures which had not been interfered with at any stage, so that they were true to life. Only in this way, he said, could photography break free from its ties with painting. Emerson also thought that photography should show us the world in the same way that our eyes did. These, according to him, produced a view which was sharp at the centre and blurred at the edges. So photographs, too, should only be in sharp focus in the middle, with the remaining areas having a softer definition. Strangely, Emerson changed his mind two years later; but, by then, it was too late, as many photographers had already taken up his suggestions.

Gathering water-lilies *by Peter Emerson (1856–1936). He gave up his medical career to become a photographer and was very influential in encouraging photographers to break away from copying painting styles.*

18

Left Fotogramm, *taken in 1930 by El Lissitzky. A student of the Bauhaus, where he was taught by Moholy-Nagy, his work was shown at 'Film und Foto' in 1929. This was a major exhibition in Stuttgart, Germany, which displayed the new directions in which photography was heading in the years between the First and Second World Wars.*

In the nineteenth century, Britain had been at the heart of all photographic activity, but in the early 1900s attention shifted across the Atlantic to the USA, and across the English Channel to Europe. Here painters had begun to experiment with new ideas and rebel against nineteenth-century traditions. The example of photography, with its tendency to freeze action and reduce movement to a blur, gave some artists the key to a new way of representing what they saw. Gradually, in the hands of groups like the Cubists, Futurists and Dadaists, ordinary objects began to lose their familiar shape and meaning and were transformed into odd new structures and forms.

Inevitably, photographers were influenced by these dramatic changes and began to interpret this new movement in their photographs. They began to use their cameras to reveal patterns and designs, in shadows and reflections, for example, that had previously been overlooked, and to take pictures from unusual angles and viewpoints. Although photographers over the years had experimented with these techniques, it was in Germany during the 1920s that this approach was explored in depth at the Bauhaus School of Art and Design. One of the teachers at the school, Laszlo Moholy-Nagy, made a particularly deep impression on the future course of photography. Combining his creative skills as a painter, sculptor, film-maker and designer, he encouraged his students to be adventurous in their photography. They experimented with collages of pictures cut out of magazines, montages combining photographs with drawn and painted images, aerial photographs, photographs with double exposures or frozen action, photograms (putting objects on to photographic paper, exposing them to light, and then processing the paper in the normal way) and solarization (quickly exposing photographic paper to light before printing a negative on to it).

Photographers in the USA were not so revolutionary. Caring little for the false attractiveness of Pictorialism, many of them turned instead to taking realistic, highly detailed pictures. New Realism was the label attached to this kind of photography, which developed after

Below Sun-bathing *taken by Laszlo Moholy-Nagy (1895–1946) around 1920. A teacher at the Bauhaus – the famous German school of art and design – he experimented with all sorts of different styles and types of photographs. The Bauhaus was closed down in 1933 and Moholy-Nagy went to the USA where he set up the New Bauhaus in Chicago. It later became the Chicago Institute of Design.*

A picture taken around 1915 by Edward Weston, when he was running a portrait studio in California. The soft, romantic image shows that he was influenced by the Pictorialist style of photography at this time.

the end of the First World War in 1918. The leader of this movement was Paul Strand, who effectively became the first important twentieth-century photographer to break away from Pictorialism. He made the decision after visiting an exhibition of Cubist work in New York. From then on, he concentrated on straightforward pictures of the everyday world, anything from a pile of bowls to New York street scenes – all of which would have been too boring and ugly for a Pictorialist.

New Realism started on the east coast of the USA but rapidly spread to the west coast, where it was adopted by Edward Weston. A keen Pictorialist who processed his photographs to look like paintings, Weston changed his style after visiting an exhibition of European modern art and then meeting Strand in New York. From the soft, manipulated photographs of Pictorialism, he switched to what he called a 'direct' approach. Subjects as wide-ranging as desert landscapes, the human body, close-ups of vegetables, weather-worn buildings and machines were captured by him in pin-sharp detail – an effect achieved by using the smallest aperture on his lens. In 1932, like-minded photographers, including Ansel Adams, joined him to form Group f64, named after the smallest aperture. Although the group soon broke up, its methods and ideas had a widespread, and long-lasting impact, contributing enormously to the development of photographic realism. Adams's powerful pictures of the Yosemite Valley, in all its natural splendour, still continue to influence people world-wide – as do his teachings on technique.

Although the main shift towards a 'straight' form of photography happened in the USA in the years between the two World Wars, there was a similar, although smaller, one in Germany. *Neue Sachlichkeit*, meaning New Objectivity, was the term used to describe German painters' interest in a more accurate and detailed approach to their

Right *In the 1920s, Edward Weston turned from Pictorialism to New Realism. Strongly influenced by the work of Paul Strand, he concentrated on creating detailed pictures of objects and landscapes to show that there is a natural beauty that can be brought to our attention through this style of photography.*

work in the mid-1920s. Their ideas soon spread to photography, where Albert Renger-Patzsch began producing pictures of everyday objects, often in close-up and with lighting that dramatized their appearance. Criticized for the cold, lifeless quality of his work, Renger-Patzsch replied that this was true photographic art, which borrowed nothing from painterly art. New Objectivity had a strong influence on European photographers, and was introduced to Britain and the USA in the 1930s, after German photographers had fled there from Nazi Germany.

By the 1930s, photography had finally broken free from the apron-strings of painting to establish its own way of looking at the world. Although painting and photography continued to be interlinked, the former could no longer dismiss the latter as a mechanical recording device over which people had little control. Developments in the USA and Germany disproved this. While Americans explored ways of showing natural and man-made objects 'in the raw', the Germans experimented with new ways of using photography, producing patterns, shapes and visual ideas which would influence the design of many things, from buildings to books, even photographs themselves.

Below *An experimental picture by Francis Bruguière, taken in the late 1920s, based around the theme of a question mark.*

4 The Selling Image

By the 1930s, photographers had proved their artistic worth: using their imagination, they had shown that all sorts of pictures could be produced. Now it was time to use their talents in the world of advertising, where so much money could be made. This was helped by the arrival in Britain and the USA of many of the staff and students

205184 MURRAY ALCOSSER
CANDY CORNS

205189 DAVID W. HAMILTON

205193 MURRAY ALCOSSER
BLUEBERRIES AND RASPBERRIES

205185 ERIC MEOLA
LIFE PRESERVER IN WATER

205194 MURRAY ALCOSSER
STRAWBERRY

205190 CLIFF FEULNER

205186 ALFRED GESCHEIDT

205195 MURRAY ALCOSSER
JELLY BEANS

TIB
THE IMAGE BANK ®

205187 CLAUDE CHASSAGNE

205191 BONNIE RAUCH

205196 GARRY GAY

Above *In the 1930s, fashion photography was theatrical and dramatic to compliment the styles of the time.*

Left *A sample page from a picture library's brochure. Advertising agencies will use images like these to help sell their customers' products. When they choose the photographs they want to use, they pay a fee to the agency for lending them the image.*

of the Bauhaus, who had fled from the rise of Nazism in Germany. The Bauhaus itself was closed in 1933 as part of the Nazis' clampdown on all artistic experimentation.

The skills and ideas of these German immigrants were welcomed by societies in which the visual communication of information and ideas, using photographs, films, and specially designed drawings and paintings, had taken over from the written word. People now wanted to 'see' things, rather than read or be told about them. In fact, the conveying of information had itself become an important industry. Both Britain and the USA were now 'consumer' societies: ones which depended on their population buying the products being made in their factories. If no one bought these, the factory owners would not have the money to replace them or to pay their workers, who then would not be able to buy the things made by other people, and so on. Firms realized that photography had a part to play in this cycle, especially as having the current fashion or style in clothes, cars, furniture etcetera became important. Not only could photography be used to advertise what was in the shops, it could even persuade people to go and buy new styles. Firms, too, required information on new machinery and processes for their factories, and were keen to inform foreign manufacturers about the products and services they could supply. What better way to communicate all this than in brochures illustrated with photographs? People, as well, wanted to tell others about themselves and a photograph spoke more than words, whether it was above the family fireplace, outside a theatre or cinema, or on the front cover of *Vogue*.

Photographs now had to do the specific job of publicizing or even selling a product or person. How photographers went about this depended on the subject. A publicity shot of a factory machine required a different approach to a portrait of a celebrity or a picture of a glamorous model. Each of these had their own photographic style, which varied almost as much as other styles in society.

During the 1930s, the powerful, factual approaches of the German New Objectivity movement and the American Group f64 were the most popular styles of photography in advertising. New Objectivity, especially, was the favourite of manufacturers. Its detailed presentation of everyday objects was ideally suited for displaying their products effectively in publications and on posters.

In portrait and fashion photography for magazines, there were two opposing styles. One moved in a 'realistic' direction, producing natural-looking pictures. Its portraits were direct and frank, often showing people at work; while in its fashion pictures, models displayed clothes and their accessories in genuine settings in preference to a studio set. The other style adopted a Pictorialist view, producing soft, dreamy pictures of people in obviously artificial surroundings. Baron Adolphe de Meyer, a famous American fashion photographer, was the master of this approach which suited the glossy image of women's magazines such as *Vogue*. In Britain, it was adopted

Film actress Katherine Hepburn, taken by Sir Cecil Beaton (1904–80). His background in the theatre as a stage and costume designer, is reflected in his photography. He is most famous for the portrait and fashion photographs he took for Vogue *magazine.*

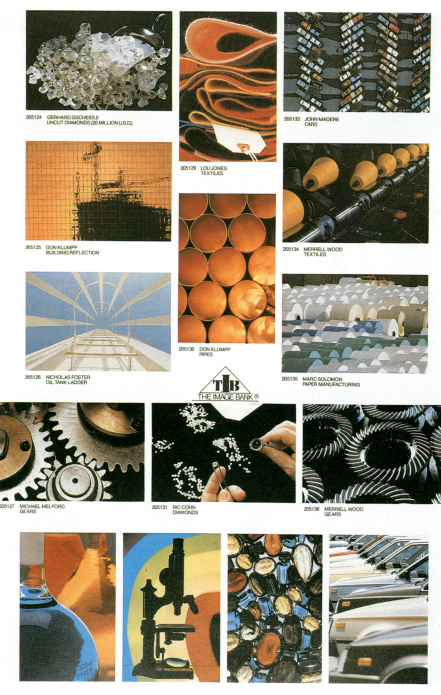

205124 GERHARD GSCHEIDLE
UNCUT DIAMONDS (20 MILLION U.S.D.)

205129 LOU JONES
TEXTILES

205133 JOHN MADERE
CARS

205125 DON KLUMPP
BUILDING REFLECTION

205134 MERRELL WOOD
TEXTILES

205126 NICHOLAS FOSTER
OIL TANK LADDER

205130 DON KLUMPP
PIPES

THE IMAGE BANK ®

205135 MARC SOLOMON
PAPER MANUFACTURING

205127 MICHAEL MELFORD
GEARS

205131 RIC COHN
DIAMONDS

205136 MERRELL WOOD
GEARS

A page from a picture library's brochure showing the exciting and colourful images than can be used to illustrate the machines and products used in industry.

by Cecil Beaton, who soon became renowned for his flamboyant portraits of people in specially built sets which reflected his training as a painter and stage designer. In the late 1930s, Angus McBean, another British photographer, introduced an experimental approach into his portraits with a series in the style of Surrealism. This had developed from the Dadaist art movement and concentrated on creating mixed-up, dream-like images of familiar objects in unusual settings. Using double exposures and montages, McBean produced odd, tongue-in-cheek pictures of famous actors.

The outbreak of the Second World War in 1939 halted any further experiments, as professional photographers were employed by their governments to take straightforward pictures of all aspects of war: the images spoke for themselves and needed no artistic assistance in getting their message over. Instead of promoting a product or a person, photographers were now employed to 'sell' a country to its people and to foreigners. Pictures of war-torn London, for instance, were sent to governments, unsure of who to join, in the hope of persuading them to side with the Allies against Germany (the Germans were doing the same thing themselves). Within all the warring nations, propaganda pictures were circulated to foster a feeling of patriotism. These pictures emphasized the positive aspects of the war in the hope of banishing any doubt from people's minds. Of course, the ultimate propaganda pictures emerged at the end of the Second World War, when Germany's concentration camps were opened up to the camera's lens. The distressing sights shocked and horrified the world, as did the equally disturbing pictures of the Allied atomic bombings of Nagasaki and Hiroshima.

The austerity of post-war years, when money and goods were limited, was reflected in a new simple and direct style of magazine photography. It started in the USA with photographers like Richard Avedon, Irving Penn and Arnold Newman, and then spread to Britain, where John French began taking pictures in the late 1950s that would show up well on the fashion pages of newspapers, which until then had relied on drawings. In doing so, he opened up a new market for fashion photography, away from such expensive women's magazines as *Vogue* and *Harper's Bazaar*. This increased the demand for fashion photographers, which rose even more in the next decade.

Above *During the Second World War (1939–45), Beaton was employed as a war photographer by the British government. He took this picture in 1942 in North Africa.*

Left *Twiggy, one of the most famous models of the 1960s, sporting the latest fashion in 1967. Compare this photograph with the one on page 22.*

25

In contrast to the 1950s, the 1960s were a boom time, with shops full of goods and pockets full of money to be spent. It was also a time when anything British was in fashion around the world, especially clothes and pop music. To be stylish was to wear British designs and listen to superstar groups like the Beatles and the Rolling Stones. The clothing and music industries rubbed their hands with glee and greed, even more so when magazines sprang up, centred around discussing their products and personalities. They were ideal channels to tempt even more people to part with their money. Inevitably, photographers became part of this, especially fashion photographers like David Bailey and Terence Donovan.

The 1960s were also a period when the emphasis was on the individual. People were freer to do what they wanted without being criticized. Boosted by this and their social acceptance and popularity, photographers had more confidence to develop their own ideas, independent of any group or movement either within photography or in the art world as a whole. This was a great contrast to 100 years earlier, when a feeling of being inferior caused photographers to join together to copy the style and ideas of painters. Indeed, photography and art merged again, each feeding off the other for ideas. Painters copied the styles of the professional magazine photographers and even used photographs as the subject of their work. Photographers, too, adopted a whole range of different approaches to their work, from those who used it to make statements about changes in society to those who regarded it as a means of looking deeply into their own personality and problems. In Britain, photography was recognized as belonging to the visual arts and began to be taught in art colleges, alongside film, painting and design. In the USA it had been taught since the late 1930s, when the Bauhaus School in Germany was shut down by the Nazis, and Lazlo Moholy-Nagy opened the 'new' Bauhaus in Chicago.

Photography's popularity spilled over into the 1970s. Photographic galleries were opened in Britain and the USA and books were produced about individual photographers' work, often by publishing firms set up by photographers. In 1972, the Arts Council in Britain decided that photography merited government subsidy and began providing money for exhibitions and projects – something the National Endowment for the Arts, in the USA, had been doing since the mid-1960s. Museums, too, decided to take an interest in photographs, displaying their own collections and making plans for their expansion. The experimentation begun in the previous decade continued in the USA as photographers looked for new ways of expressing themselves. In Europe, on the other hand, they began to look back to one of the oldest roles of a photographer – the documentary photographer, who is responsible for supplying a record of social and political situations, with the aim of conveying information with a message. It is this aspect of photography that we will look at next.

Inset *Sir Cecil Beaton continued to create memorable pictures late in his life. Here is a portrait of the American artist Andy Warhol and friend taken in 1969.*

Right *Photographs, like this one, are used in glossy holiday brochures to advertise luxurious resorts and entice people to travel abroad.*

5 The Telling Image

From its early days, photography has been respected for its truthfulness – its ability to supply an accurate picture of a person or a place: something that seemed far more real than even the most detailed description in writing or lifelike drawing or painting. You may never have met the person or visited the place, but after seeing the photograph you know *exactly* what they both look like.

The same cannot be said of writing and painting, both of which can be used to describe people and places that do not exist. Writers and painters can create stories and pictures from their imaginations. They can portray an unreal world that only exists on paper or canvas. Writers and painters can terrify us with ghosts and vampires; photographers cannot.

However, photographers can shock in other ways; simply by using their pictures to show us the world as it is. These pictures belong to 'documentary photography', the branch of photography concerned with communicating information about people and their lives. Early documentary photographers had great difficulty selling pictures of everyday life, especially of the poorer areas of towns and cities, because people were not interested in what was going on around them. However, as housing and working conditions worsened in the wake of the Industrial Revolution, British social reformers began to use photographers to help draw attention to these terrible situations. The pictures that John Thomson published in his *Street Life in London* in 1877 had much more impact than the written word. Now people could actually *see* what had been described in words, and conditions were frequently much worse than they had previously imagined.

The USA was the home of documentary photography in the late nineteenth and early twentieth centuries. There, in the 1880s, Edward S. Curtis began photographing the lives of the remaining North American Indians, who had been brutally driven off their lands into reservations by European settlers. Later, Jacob Riis, a journalist in New York in the 1890s, wrote angrily about the conditions in the city's slums and schools. His words had little effect on his readers, so he took up photography to make his point more forcefully. His pictures were used in pamphlets and exhibitions and led to some of the worst slum buildings in New York being pulled down and more money being spent on the city's schools.

Encouraged by Riis's success, the National Child Labor Committee employed Lewis Hine to take photographs of children working in factories as part of their campaign to abolish such exploitation. He travelled all over the USA, often risking his life to obtain material,

Right *A picture of an Apache chief and his family taken by Edward S. Curtis as part of a survey of native American life in North America. Begun in 1896, the task occupied him until 1930, during which time he took over 40,000 photographs. The best of these were published in a twenty-volume book entitled* The North American Indian.

Below *An old woman in the slums of New York, taken by Jacob Riis (1849– 1914) around 1890. Determined to improve living conditions in the city, Riis gave up journalism in favour of photography because he realized that pictures would have a greater impact than the written word.*

Photographs, like this one, had great impact when they were first published. This was taken by Dorothea Lange (1895–1965) in 1936, when she was working for the Farm Security Administration in Oklahoma. This mother and her children are preparing to start a new life in California after having their lives ruined by drought and dust storms.

which was used to illustrate the Committee's publications. Hine carried on his work into the 1930s, when a law was eventually passed, banning the employment of children in factories.

By then, the USA had entered the dark days of an economic slump, brought on by the collapse of share prices in 1929. Farmers were particularly hard hit and many went bankrupt. Already weakened financially, those in the central states soon had to confront another disaster. A prolonged drought, from 1932 to 1936, turned their lands into a dust bowl. Unable to cope any more, many left their homes and began the long trek to the green valleys of California in search of a better life. Such was the scale of the problem that the government set up the Farm Security Administration (FSA) in the mid-1930s to help the farmers find new homes and jobs. The FSA decided to use photographers to help keep a record of its work. Over the next few years, teams were sent out to take pictures of the drought-stricken areas and the families that were forced to leave their homes. What they came back with shocked the nation and moved John Steinbeck to write his powerful novel *The Grapes of Wrath*.

News magazines, illustrated with photographs, arrived in America in the mid-1930s and helped the FSA's photographers get their message across to a wider audience. Their pictures initially took second place to the articles; but such was their effect on the readers that they quickly became more important. These magazines had started in Germany in the late 1920s, at a time when she led the world in printing techniques and camera design. In 1925, a German company produced the Leica, a small camera that was to become the indispensable tool of a new breed of documentary photographer: the photojournalist.

In the new magazines, photographers were given several pages to tell a story through pictures. In effect, the pictures took the place of words written by a journalist, so this type of story was called photojournalism. In the same way that a journalist was allowed to express an opinion in his or her writing, the photojournalist could use pictures to make a point. In magazines and newspapers, there were editors to prepare a journalist's story for publication, cutting it if it was too long, livening it up if it was too boring and drawing the reader's attention to it with a snappy headline. These were people who thought of a page in terms of words. People were now needed who thought visually. Picture editors became responsible for choosing the pictures and deciding how they should be laid out on the pages. In the same way that an editor could improve a written article by chopping and changing it, so a picture editor could alter the appearance of a picture story through the selection and layout of photographs.

The political situation in Germany in the early 1930s disturbed many of the staff working on the picture magazines in that country and they emigrated to Britain and the USA. Here, they helped to set up magazines similar to the ones they had just left. The most famous were *Life*, which started in the USA in 1936, followed by *Picture Post*

(1938) and *Illustrated* (1939) in Britain. In the days before television, these magazines were an important source of news and views and greatly influenced their readers' opinions on all sorts of matters. Their photographers became celebrities, becoming known to millions with their stories from all corners of the globe. At one point, it was estimated that 30 million people read each issue of *Life*.

The spread of television during the 1950s led to a decline in the number of people reading these magazines, forcing *Picture Post* to close in 1957 and *Illustrated* in 1958. *Life* carried on until 1972, when it, too, ceased publication. By then, photojournalism had lost much of the power it once had. It still existed in Europe in magazines like *Stern* (West German) and *Paris Match* (French), and in the colour supplements accompanying British newspapers, but in a weaker form. Newspapers, of course, used photographs for some of their articles, but perhaps only half a dozen pictures for a major story;

Picture Post, February 22, 1941 Registered at the G.P.O. as a Newspaper

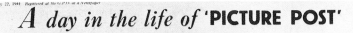

A day in the life of 'PICTURE POST'

Here comes "Picture Post" through the letter-box. It's a funny thing but young Tony is generally down early on a Wednesday and he's on to it like a flash.

Tony can't read all "Picture Post" before breakfast. But this morning he's lucky — Dad has a letter from the Income Tax which demands his undivided attention. For once, he goes off to town without his copy of "Picture Post."

Mother finds the "Picture Post" when she's dusting. Over her eleven o'clock cup of tea, she has a good dip into it — almost forgets the time.

After lunch, Dora the maid finds it. She dreams over it, while the washing-up water gets cold.

Daphne gets home from her A.R.P. duty and she's in a hot bath, reading "Picture Post," as fast as she can make it.

Daphne leaves "Picture Post" in the bathroom. The plumber who's come in to put new washers on the taps reads it during his tea break.

Dad arrives home and after dinner he makes himself thoroughly comfortable for an hour with "Picture Post."

Dad's gone to the Home Guard — and taken "Picture Post" with him. His corporal is very glad he did. He says when you're on all night, you want something to read.

And there in the guardroom we leave "Picture Post." It's going to start a new cycle of life tomorrow. It will be going on for months to come — you never see "Picture Post" thrown away.

Read **POST** *in comfort — order it at home*

A page from Picture Post, *the most famous of the British picture magazines. Note that words take second place to the photographs: the pictures tell the story, not the words. Picture Post was first published in 1938 and lasted until 1957.*

31

whereas a picture magazine might devote fifteen to twenty pages to photographs. Many photojournalists now switched to travel, personality portraits, sport and similar specialist areas. This material could be sold over and over again to book and magazine publishers, which were using an increasing number of photographs.

A regular feature in *Life* in its last few years was the war in Vietnam. Often referred to as the world's first 'media war', because of the enormous coverage it received in print and on film, some of the most memorable images have been those captured by stills photographers. War photography is almost as old as photography itself and is another offshoot of documentary photography. The first war photographer was Roger Fenton, who went to the Crimea in 1855 to take pictures of British troops fighting against the Russians. Judged by today's standards, the 360 photographs he brought back are tame and contain little of the unpleasantness of battle. In contrast, Mathew Brady's coverage of the American Civil War (1861–65) was more realistic and included pictures of dead soldiers. These early war photographers were hindered by their cumbersome equipment. This was not the case for those of the next century. Photographers like Robert Capa and Don McCullin have risked their lives to provide us with frontline pictures from war zones all round the world, frequently in gruesome, graphic detail. Unpleasant they may be but, in the true spirit of documentary photography, therein lies the message.

The documentary photographer must have the talent to capture the right moment, whether it is death, despair or delight. Some of this is due to being in the right place at the right time but even so, deciding on the angle which will produce the most telling image, requires imagination and good judgement. There is little point in trying to convey a message unless it is done in the most powerful manner possible, for only then will people sit up and take note.

Above *A picture taken by* Picture Post *photographer Haywood Magee as part of an assignment she was doing on the flood of West Indian immigrants who arrived in Britain in 1956. Stories on social issues, like this one, played an important part in this magazine.*

Inset *Mathew Brady (1823–96) by the side of his travelling darkroom. He organized teams of photographers to cover all aspects of the American Civil War (1861–65). In all, about 7,000 pictures were taken. Although Brady took some, the bulk were supplied by his employees.*

Right *A picture taken by Robert Capa in Germany on the day the Second World War ended in 1945. He called it* The Last Man to Die. *He was the most famous war photographer of the 1930s and 1940s, much of his work being published in* Life *magazine. Born in 1914, he was killed in 1954 on a battlefield in South-east Asia.*

6 The Visible Invisible

We have just been looking at the way in which photographers show us the world we can see: let us now look at how the camera can be used to provide us with pictures of the world we cannot see.

The human eye is a very limited device for observing what is going on around us. It can only function in light and only within a narrow range of brightness, because it is difficult to see things if the light is too bright or too dim.

Objects must move at the right speed for our eyes to pick them up. Anything that travels faster than about one-tenth of a second is too quick: at best, it may be seen as a blur, such as a jet fighter roaring past; at worst, not at all, as in the case of a bullet fired by a gun.

Conversely, changes taking place over hours, days or weeks occur too slowly. We cannot concentrate on them for such lengths of time, so they pass unnoticed. Objects must also be of a certain size before our eyes can spot them.

A great deal happens in the world which we do not know about, just because of the way in which our eyes have been designed. We use our eyes to pick up energy called light that is transmitted on a certain wavelength. The correct name for light is 'visible radiation'. Energy that is transmitted on other wavelengths, for instance radiation in the form of X-rays or infra-red rays, cannot be picked up by our eyes so they cannot be seen – they are invisible. But they can be picked up on films whose chemicals are sensitive to invisible radiation, from which we can obtain a photograph. Light, because of its wavelength, cannot pass through many substances, whereas invisible radiation, of a shorter or longer wavelength, can. By using these wavelengths, we can obtain photographs of things we cannot normally see.

The use of invisible radiation in photography has opened up a whole new world. Radiography, for example, uses the penetrative power of X-rays and gamma rays to look for cracks inside machines or pipes and to diagnose illnesses within the human body. Thermography uses the heat-carrying wavelengths of infra-red radiation to produce pictures of the heat emitted by objects. In medicine, such pictures are used to detect cancerous tumours, because the diseased areas are colder than the surrounding healthy parts. Engineers can take thermographic photographs of buildings to track down the areas where heat is escaping, so that they know where insulation is needed. Aerial thermographs can be taken of farmland to reveal the crops affected by pests, as healthy crops give off more heat than damaged ones. Farmers can then quickly decide which fields need to be sprayed with chemicals and pesticides and which do not.

Right *A fifteen-week-old human foetus photographed inside the womb – just one of the many leaps forward in photography in recent years.*

Below *A thermographic photograph of a house. The red areas show where heat is escaping from the inside, indicating where insulation is needed.*

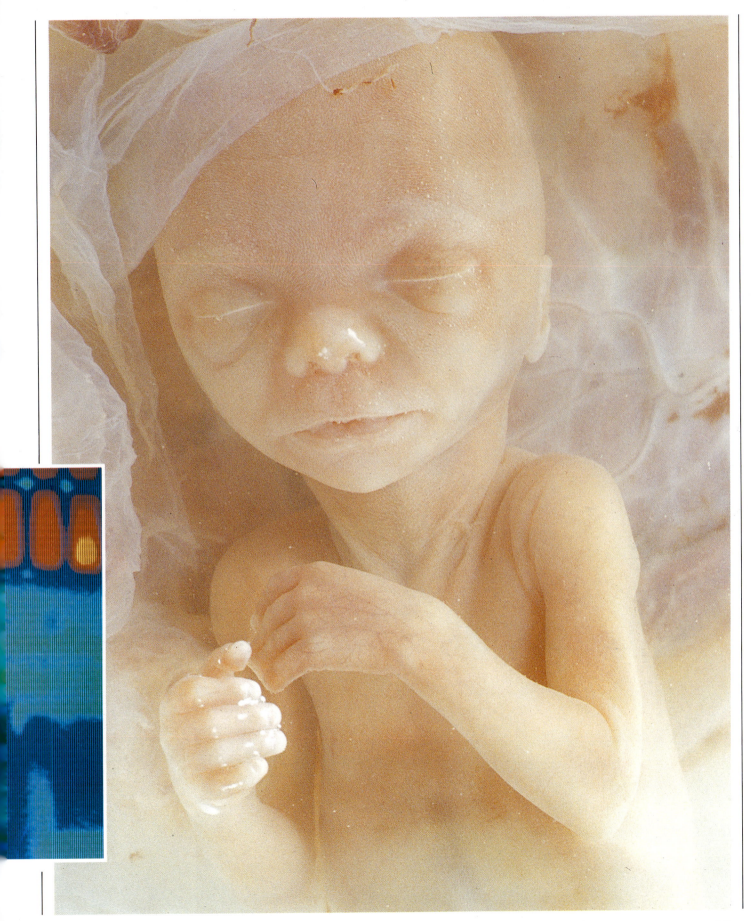

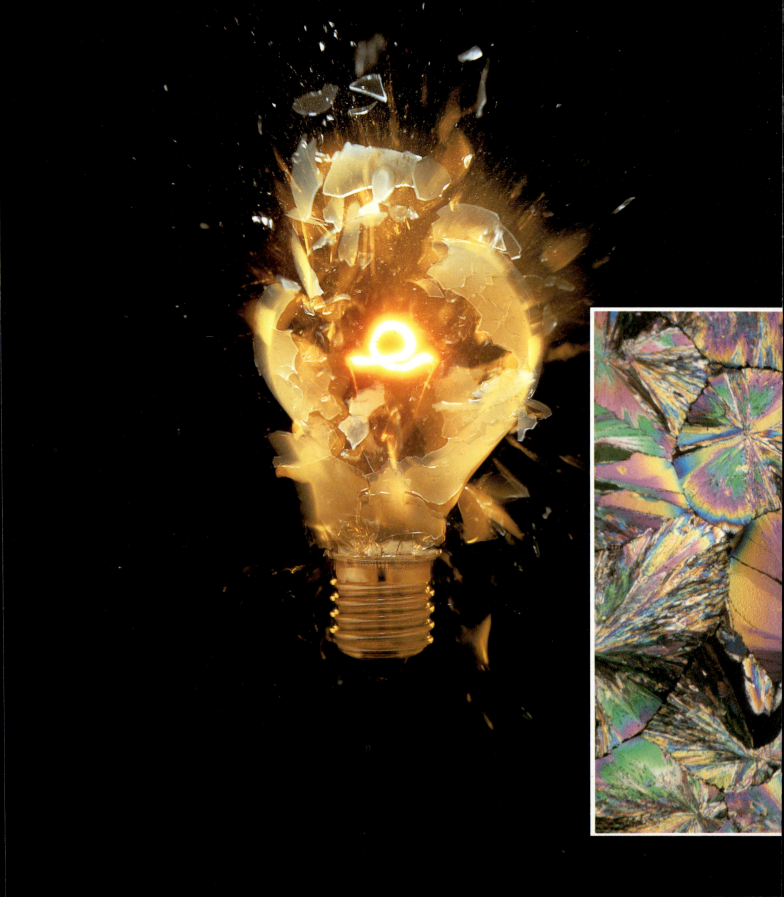

Invisible radiation can also be used to reveal the contents of darkest space. Once again, a normal film would be of little use here as there is no visible radiation. However, pictures can be made with the help of films sensitive to different wavelengths and then sent back to earth. This is no problem if the spacecraft containing the cameras is returning, but increasingly they are being sent on one-way journeys deep into the universe. Here, the answer is to replace the conventional camera with one that picks up invisible radiation and then records it electronically, and not on film. The information can then be changed into another wavelength, radio signals, and beamed back to earth. Here, computers are used to convert the signals into information that can be displayed on a television screen and the image is photographed by a camera.

The camera can also record movements that are too fast for the human eye to catch. This is called high-speed photography, not only because it deals with motion, but also because a fast shutter speed is required (one that lets light into the camera for only a very short time) to freeze the action. This technique was pioneered by Eadweard Muybridge in the USA in the 1870s. His sequence of pictures freezing a galloping horse proved that horses did lift all four hooves off the ground, something that people had refused to believe until confronted by the evidence. Today, scientists use this type of photography to analyze explosions, experiments and everyday occurrences, such as what happens to an egg when it hits the floor. Naturalists also use it to investigate the actions of birds or insects in flight, capturing movements too quick to be understood by the human eye.

The opposite of high-speed photography is time-lapse photography. Here, by using either a very long exposure (leaving the shutter open for some time) or taking pictures at repeated intervals over a period, developments too slow for our eyes to see can be captured and studied. This method can be used, for example, to show a bud forming on a plant and then opening into a flower.

Finally, the camera can reveal a world that is far too small for our eyes to notice: the world of photomicrography. The simplest way of achieving this is to attach a camera to a microscope, but even this method cannot penetrate into the miniscule territory of, say, a living cell, which needs to be enlarged 250,000 times before it can be seen. To picture something as small as this, an electron microscope is needed. When charged up with several thousand volts of electricity, electrons behave like light of very short wavelength, which can be focused on an object by electromagnets, in the same way that a glass lens focuses light in a camera. The image produced appears on a television screen, which can then be photographed. Until 1942, the presence of viruses to account for certain illnesses was a matter of debate among the medical profession. In that year, however, their existence was confirmed by a photograph taken through an electron microscope. This is just one example of this form of photography's importance in the development of science.

⑦ Taking Pictures

How a camera works.

A camera is really only a box with a hole, called the aperture, at one end and a light-sensitive film at the other. In between, there is a lens and a shutter. The lens acts as a magnifying glass, concentrating the rays of light passing through the aperture on to the film and stopping them bouncing all round the inside of the camera. The shutter opens and closes, letting light in or keeping it out. Photography is all about how much light strikes the film, and for what length of time. How much light comes into the camera depends on the size of the aperture, which can be altered from a wide hole to a pinprick. The length of time light lands on the film depends on how long the shutter remains open, which can vary from several seconds to tiny fractions of a second.

Exposure.

For every picture there is only one correct aperture and shutter setting. This combination is called the exposure. There are 'long' exposures and 'short' exposures. A long exposure, as it implies, means that the shutter is open for the best part of a second or more and a short exposure, for merely a fraction of that time. In a long exposure, since the light is allowed into the camera for a long time, only a small amount is needed, so the aperture is a pinprick. Conversely, with a short exposure, a lot of light is needed to strike the film for a small amount of time, so the aperture is much larger.

Left *Photographs not only convey information, but also moods. Beautiful images can be created using, in this case, a natural landscape, with the use of special lenses and filters.*

Picture sharpness.

In most manual cameras, the position of the lens can be altered, backwards or forwards, to allow you to take pictures of objects nearby or in the distance. Making sure that these objects show up sharply in your picture is called focusing. The sharpness of a picture can also be affected by the size of the aperture: the smaller it is, the sharper the whole of your picture will be. With a large aperture, only a small area, just in front of, and behind the object you have focused on, will be sharp. The part of your picture that is detailed and sharp is called the depth of field. With a large aperture, there is a small depth of field and with a small aperture, there is a large depth of field.

Below *To get a sharp, detailed picture like this, you have got to hold the camera steady or use a tripod. Note, too, how the flags draw your eyes into the centre of the picture, to the eyes on this Nepalese temple's spire. This is called good composition.*

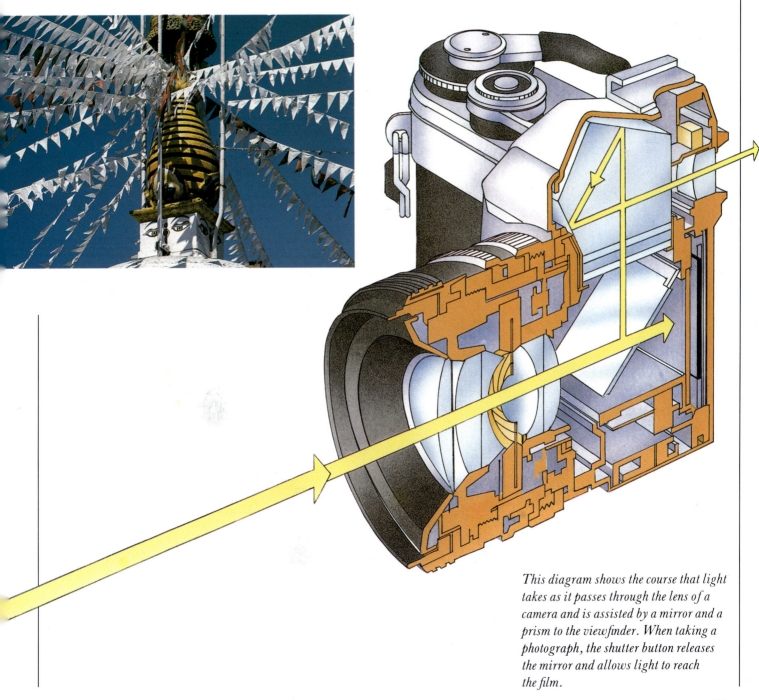

This diagram shows the course that light takes as it passes through the lens of a camera and is assisted by a mirror and a prism to the viewfinder. When taking a photograph, the shutter button releases the mirror and allows light to reach the film.

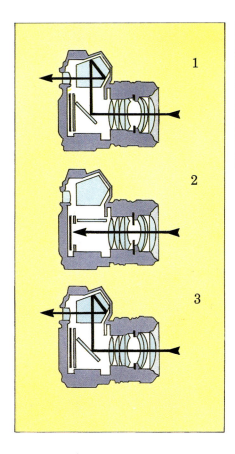

1. Light passes through the lens at full aperture and is reflected by the mirror into the pentaprism and then the viewfinder.

2. Pressing the shutter button releases the mirror and allows the light to pass through the shutter to the film. The aperture adjusts to the required setting.

3. After releasing the shutter button, the mirror drops down again and the aperture returns to its largest setting.

Modern, automatic SLR cameras mean that anyone can take a picture like this – with a bit of practice! Only a few years ago, only a professional would have had the equipment to do so.

Camera types.
There are many different types of camera to choose from today. These range from simple automatic models, to the complex and advanced manual cameras used by professional photographers. If you just want to take photographs of holidays and friends, there is a large choice of reasonably-priced, easy-to-use automatic cameras on the market. However, if you want more control over your camera and are keen to learn about photography, then a single lens reflex (SLR) camera is the

type of model you should buy. Special lenses, filters and motors can be bought that fix on to SLR cameras, so that at the least, you will have a fairly simple manual camera, and at the most a camera capable of a wide range of photographic techniques.

There is a large selection of SLR cameras to choose from. The amount of money that you can afford to spend will narrow your choice. Look in photographic magazines and camera shops for advice on which model you should buy.

Lenses.

Most SLRs are sold with a 50 mm lens. This is called a 'standard' lens because it provides a picture of the view that is very similar to what the eye sees. Lenses smaller than this, the 35 mm, or 28 mm, for example, have a wider range of view than the human eye, so they are called wide-angle lenses. Lenses larger than the 50 mm are called telephoto lenses, because they make an object appear bigger than it is in real life, and bring it closer to the camera. Which type of lens you buy depends on what you use your camera for. If you enjoy taking pictures of wildlife or sports people in action, then a telephoto would be the most useful. If you prefer photographing landscapes, then a wide-angle would be better. In fact, nowadays, choosing a lens needn't be a problem as you can buy just one, a 'zoom' lens, that ranges from 35 to 200 mm. Another factor to bear in mind when thinking about lenses is sharpness. The longer the lens, the less sharp the picture. Conversely, the smaller the lens, the sharper the picture. This is because smaller lenses have a greater depth of field.

Films.

Most cameras now use 35 mm film, and the majority of people load them with colour film. This is available for colour prints or colour transparencies (the correct name for slides). Unless you own a projector and screen for viewing transparencies, it is better to use print films. These have different ISO numbers, (formerly known as ASA numbers) which show how sensitive each film is to light. The lower the ISO number, the brighter the light needs to be for that film. The higher the number, the duller the light should be. So a film with an ISO of 200 needs less light than a film with an ISO of 100. Which type of film you buy depends a great deal on the weather. If you are going to take pictures on a sunny day, in bright light, you need a film with a low ISO number, like 100; but on a grey day, when there is little light, you will want a film with a higher ISO number such as 200 or even 400. Another point to bear in mind is that the higher the ISO number, the grainer will be the picture: a print from an ISO 400 film will appear fuzzier and less sharp than one from an ISO 100. You might not notice the difference on a normal-size print, but it will be more obvious on prints that you enlarge to a bigger size. So if you are planning on enlarging some of your pictures, it's better to use a film with a low ISO number.

The top picture was taken with a wide-angle lens (28mm) and the one below it with a telephoto lens (200mm). Both were taken from the same position, but notice how the area of the subject changes.

The correct way to hold a camera: feet apart, elbows tucked into your chest and lens supported by your free hand. Relax, compose your picture and then press the shutter button gently and smoothly.

Taking a good photograph.

It is important, when taking photographs, to think about certain factors, that combined, are the basic ingredients of a good picture: an eye-catching subject, a little thought and imagination, patience and a thorough knowledge of the camera you are using. Before taking a picture, stop and think about what you are taking before pressing the shutter button. If you do this and take the following advice you will be amazed at how easy it is to turn a boring snap into an exciting photograph.

- **Know your camera.** Read through the instruction book carefully, then practise, using the camera you have bought without a film inside, until you know what all the knobs and dials are for and can set them without thinking.

- **Keep it clean.** Make sure the lens and the inside of the camera are free of dirt and dust at all times. When you buy your camera, make sure you have a blower brush and special lens tissues to keep the camera clean. Many people keep a clear 'skylight' filter over their lenses to protect them from dirt and scratches.

- **Keep the camera steady.** Support it with one hand under the lens; the other grasping the side next to the shutter button. Stand with your feet apart, hold your breath for a second and press the shutter button gently and smoothly. If the shutter is going to be open for longer than one sixtieth of a second, support the camera on a tripod or a flat, firm surface.

- **Keep it level.** Make sure that vertical and horizontal lines match those of the base and sides of the viewfinder, so that people and buildings do not tumble out of your picture down a sloping horizon.

- **Keep it simple.** There is no need to clutter up a picture with too many subjects. A simple image is usually more effective.

- **Be selective.** Choose the best angle for a picture. If you are not happy with what you see in the viewfinder, do not press the button. Go in closer, move back, kneel down, climb higher, or walk round a subject until you like what you see.

- **Be adventurous.** Use different effects in your photographs, such as filters, varying the depth of field, blurring instead of freezing action, and odd angles. As you have seen in this book, photography can be combined with other art forms to create fascinating pictures.

- **Be critical.** Analyze your mistakes to find out where you went wrong so that they are not repeated.

- **Never be satisfied.** Never be content with what you know: there is always more to learn. Read magazines and books to see what other photographers are up to. Talk to other photographers and try to get some useful tips from them.

- **Have fun.** If you enjoy what you are doing, you are far more likely to take good pictures.

Above *Simple subjects, with bold colours, make very effective photographs.*

Right *This special effect was achieved by 'zooming' a telephoto lens while the picture was being taken.*

Further Information

Career Information

Magazines are a very useful source of all manner of information, from the present state of the industry to tips on getting the most from your camera. Most of them have letters pages, answering readers' problems. Some have clubs which organize photographic holidays and courses, and even arrange price reductions for their members with camera shops. Many of the large camera manufacturers, too, have a club for people who use their equipment, which publishes a magazine and runs competitions. You may also consider joining a local camera club, where you can meet other photographers, enter competitions to see what they think of your efforts, and perhaps have access to darkroom facilities to learn about developing, processing and printing your films. Your nearest reference library should have details of all the clubs in your area. It will also have a collection of historical photographs of local people and places, where you can see the work of early photographers. Finally, keep an eye open for any exhibitions near you. These are usually free and display all types of photographs, which will give you ideas on how you can improve your own techniques.

There are a wide variety of opportunities for a photographer to earn a living. If you are keen and dedicated, one of the following options could be yours.

Most students of photography dream about becoming famous fashion photographers like Norman Parkinson or David Bailey, but only a very few make it. However, there are many other areas that are interesting and well paid, including advertising from fashion to industry; press photography for newspapers and magazines; wedding and portrait photography; medical and scientific photography, and taking photographs for the police.

Most of today's professional photographers began as assistants in photographic studios. Many would have studied photography at college and before that have been members of photographic clubs. Look out for the nearest club in your area, and find out which colleges offer a course in practical and technical photography. Jobs for assistants in professional studios are advertised in the back of many photographic magazines. Lastly, photography is a highly competitive business so you will need to work extremely hard and commit yourself totally to this exciting industry.

Glossary

Aperture The hole controlling the amount of light which passes through a camera's lens and on to the film.

Camera obscura A darkened room with a small hole in either the ceiling or one wall, through which light can pass to form an image of the scene outside on the opposite wall or on a table below.

Chemical reaction The process in which a substance changes colour or form (from a liquid to a gas, for example) as a result of the action of heat, light or the presence of another substance.

Collodion This sticky solution of ether and alcohol was discovered in 1847 and used for dressing wounds in the Crimean War. In the 1850s photographers began to use it in photography.

Daguerreotype process The photographic method invented by Louis Daguerre and revealed to the world in 1839. It produced a positive image on a polished metal plate.

Double exposure The technique of taking more than one picture on a single frame of film. The resulting photograph, when developed, will have several images on it.

Gamma rays Invisible energy given off by certain substances.

Gelatin A natural protein which can be used to stick light-sensitive chemicals to paper or film.

Group f64 An important group of American photographers of the 1930s, including Ansel Adams and Edward Weston. They concentrated on taking very sharp, detailed pictures by using the smallest aperture on their lenses. The size of an aperture is called its 'f' number: the bigger this is, the smaller is the aperture and the sharper the picture will be. The smallest aperture the group used on their lenses was f64, so this was the name they gave themselves.

Industrial Revolution The expansion of industry which used machines in the early nineteenth century.

Montage A picture made up from several other ones, arranged so that they join, overlap or blend with one another.

Negative An image in which the light areas appear dark and the dark areas light. A negative is usually made of a transparent substance so that light can pass through it on to photographic paper to produce a positive image.

New Objectivity A style of photography which started in Germany in the 1920s. The photographers who practised it, produced very detailed, straightforward pictures of everyday objects and scenes.

New Realism Another name for New Objectivity.

Photojournalism Journalism that uses photographs to tell a news story, more than the written word.

Pictorialism A style of photography in which a photograph's attractiveness is more important than conveying information about its subject.

Plates Originally this meant the light-sensitive copper plates used by Daguerre. From the 1850s, however, when collodion allowed the use of glass, it referred to the glass sheets that were coated with chemicals.

Positive An image, on paper or film, in which light and dark areas are the same as the eye sees. A positive image, in colour or black and white, produced on a transparent film is called a 'transparency', often referred to as a 'slide'. The tones and colours of a positive are opposite to those of a negative.

Pre-Raphaelite Brotherhood A group of nineteenth-century British artists who painted in the style of fifteenth-century Italian painters.

Print In photography, a picture produced by light acting on photographic paper.

Radiography A photographic process where an image is produced by radiation, on special photographic film, usually by X-rays or gamma rays.

Shutter An opaque shield that opens momentarily when a photograph is taken, to admit light onto the film to capture the image that is seen through the viewfinder.

Silver chloride A chemical combination of silver and chlorine.

Silver nitrate A chemical combination of silver and nitric acid.

Thermography Pictures that are taken using the heat of infra-red energy to photograph the heat in houses, crops, the human body etc.

Further Reading

1000 Photo Tips (Pan, 1984)

The Complete Encyclopaedia of Photography by MICHAEL LANGFORD (Ebury Press, 1982)

The First Photography Book by PETER SMITH (Guinness, 1987)

History of Art for Young People by H.W. JANSON (Thames & Hudson, 1982)

History of Photography by PETER TURNER (Hamlyn Bison, 1987)

The New 35 mm Photographer's Handbook by JULIAN CALDER and JOHN GARRETT (Pan, 1986)

Pictures on a Page by HAROLD EVANS (Heinemann, 1978)

A Short History of the Camera by JOHN WADE (Fountain Press, 1979)

The Story of Photography by MICHAEL LANGFORD (Focal Press, 1980)

Picture acknowledgements

The publishers would like to thank the following for supplying the photographs for this book: Barnaby's Picture Library 22 (right); BBC Hulton Picture Library 8, 9 (top), 10, 11, 12, 16, 17 (top), 17 (bottom), 18, 25 (bottom), 28–9, 29, 30, 31, 32, 33 (inset); Bruce Coleman 7 (left), 43 (top); David Cumming 39, 41 (top & bottom), 42; John Hillelson 13, 33; Nikon 7 (right); Colin Osman 5, 19 (bottom), 19 (top), 20, 21 (bottom), 21 (top), 23, 25 (top), 27 (inset); Paul Seheult 22 (left), 24; Wayland 9 (bottom); ZEFA 4–5, 6, 14, 15 (both), 27, 34–5, 35, 36 (left), 36–7, 38, 40, 43 (bottom).
The diagrams on pages 38 and 40 were supplied by Malcolm Walker.

Index